Won't Do it!

Your guide to

Health, Freedom and Happiness

Per Nygaard

Per Nygaard

Won't Do It!

Translation: Tina Robinson/ www.actionart.dk

Cover: bettinabjals.com

Publisher: Books on Demand GmbH, Copenhagen, Denmark

Printed: Books on Demand GmbH, Norderstedt, Germany

ISBN 978-87-7145-763-6

Second edition 2014

Table of Contents

About the Author

Per Nygaard (born 1969) has been working with personal development and training of body, mind and spirit since the first time he was introduced to the martial arts world at the age of six. He has a black belt in several different martial arts systems and now runs his own training center, where he not only works as a martial arts instructor but also as a shiatsu massage practitioner and meditation teacher. Per is an active lecturer and holds many workshops. Per is committed to teaching and motivating people in personal growth and development.

www.pernygaard.dk

"Every great dream

Begins with a dreamer

Always remember

You have within you

The strength

The patience

And the passion

To reach for the stars

To change the world"

-Harriet Tubman

The Essence

Before we get to the preface, I would quickly like
to talk about the essence of this book. It is a sort of
service for those of you who never finish a book....

My goal with this book is not to tell you what health,
freedom and happiness is – this is and should be an
individual matter. My wish, in actuality, is to awaken
an interest in you. An interest in you, yourself,
choosing to take responsibility for your life and your
dreams; that you find self worth and courage enough
to follow your goals so they don't become wasted
chances and lost possibilities which risk, in the end,
leading you to fiasco and/or illness.

The first thing you need to do is find the desire and
energy to really want to fulfill your innermost dreams.
You must create your own life philosophy which
supports you no matter what challenges may come
your way. In order to have something to go for, it is
important that you know precisely what your dreams
are. Moreover, they should be so big that they always
give you the desire to continue despite any hardships
that you meet on your journey.

Energy is movement, so keep on moving. Move both physically and emotionally. Shift your opinions and attitudes. Don't stand still, because if you do, the energy stops and you lose the belief in both your dreams and yourself. Practice feeling the energy in everything you do. Steer towards the good energy and move away from the bad.

You are created in a universe where co-operation is the key. You cannot do everything yourself no matter how stubborn and persistent you choose to be. You have to acknowledge that you are a part of a developing community. Otherwise, you risk burning the candle at both ends and, in the end, experiencing defeat, stress and suffering.

Patience, co-operation and presence of mind will lead you closer to your dreams coming true. You will experience that even though life can be full of challenges, stress and maybe even life threatening disease, you will always be able to find that which lifts you up and fills you with joy. And you will find out that it's not only the goal that's important, but more importantly, the path to the goal. As a wise man once said:

It's not what you do, it's how you do it!

It's not really that difficult, this thing about health and happiness for the body and soul. With just a few simple adjustments here and there, we know very well what we need to do.

In actuality, I am sure that most of us have the knowledge it takes to live a healthy and happy life. It is probably much more a question of how we mobilise that energy we need to achieve the results we want, than it is a lack of information which causes nothing to happen.

We don't get wholesome and healthy by reading about exercising and nutritious food. We don't get rich either by reading a money magazine. It's about making a decision and acting in accordance with it.

This book guides you through different phases which we experience with our body, mind and spirit. It can be that you already know a lot about the subject, but there are always new ways of understanding familiar words, if you stay open without judging.

The first part of the book describes how thoughts, habits and patterns have become controlling factors in our lives, while the second part consists, among other things, of a list of practical exercises. These exercises should be relatively easy to integrate into your life and are meant as an inspiration for changing unsuitable behavioral patterns. They can be a big help on your way to a greater self-development: better health, more freedom and a happier life.

I am convinced that everyone has tried to set a goal. We have all tried to fulfill some great idea or other that we later had to give up because we either weren't ready, weren't so sure about it being our goal anyway, or because we simply lost interest along the way. But, maybe there is a way you just haven't tried yet: One that guides you towards your goal without having to fight like crazy each and every day; a way where your deepest dreams reveal themselves to you in a tempo which you choose yourself.

To go a new way means changing focus. To change focus means that you have to remove the habits and behavioral patterns which, so far, haven't supported you in reaching your goals, and until now, have given you precisely the opposite of what you've dreamt of. This is the background on which I have chosen to write this book.

So why in the world be so passionate about personal development and growth? Why not just walk along

Life's highway and see where it leads you? Sheer chance and coincidence show us the right direction... Or do they?

My personal experience with Life's path is that even if we don't take responsibility, the path will be revealed to us. It will be revealed, not by coincidence, but as complete, structured patterns that mirror our own patterns of

behavior. So whether or not we take the bull by the horns our lives will be very precisely arranged, not by fate, but as a result of our thoughts, habits and behavioural patterns.

Today you can find so much knowledge and so many precedents of different people having achieved what they dreamt of just by making small changes in their habits. It's more the small steps we take every day, rather than our daydreams about what we could and should be doing, that bring us closer to our dreams.

When I first discovered that I could be master of my own fate, I got busy studying and reading about all the other people who knew about and practiced this already.

"Won't do it" is many years of study and experience put into one book. It's not written as if it's the absolute truth. It is meant as an appetiser on how to get going yourself with taking responsibility and testing your limits, so that your goals and dreams become a reality.

There is nothing new in this book, no secrets. Everything that is written here has been discovered by many others before me. I have just put it together using my own experiences and understanding.

I hope this book will inspire and motivate you into action. I believe that you will fulfill your dreams and desires for your own unique life.

Enjoy!

Per Nygaard

Skælskør 2013

My Story

It all began one winter day in february, 1969, when I came into this world at a little country hospital. My parents, my older sister, big brother and I, lived on a little farm out in the country. When I was about 3 months old we moved to a much bigger farm with a lot of land and quite a few more animals. I have my first memory from there when I was about to and a half years old. When I was three my parents split up. I can remember bits and pieces of my life from before they left each other and pretty much everything afterwards. After they got divorced, my brother and I moved in with our father and his new wife. I don't remember anything bad about the divorce. It was almost as if it was just a natural thing that happened in my youth.

During the next four years we moved around quite a few times. A short time after that my father and his wife got divorced. At that point, we had moved back to the country into an old, run down cottage with a little barn and some land. My father was, and still is, the type who always had a lot of projects going at the same time. This time it was the project called, "rebuilding of very old crap into a really nice place." We always helped with cleaning up, repairing various things, taking care of the animals and the fields and so on. We, my brother and I, became very good at fixing all kinds of things. I have often teased my father that at the tender age of 12 I was a trained carpenter, gardener, bricklayer, painter and farmer. These are some of the abilities that I am very happy to have today.

It was while my father was without a partner that I started to get acquainted with martial arts. Every now and again my father had evening shifts at the boys home where he worked. That meant that my brothers and I would be babysat by Allan. Allan was a young guy of about 20 and he studied karate. On the days that he took care of us we trained martial arts in our living room. I really got into it and even though it was only eight to ten times that it happened, a seed was sown in me which, today, still grows.

My father got married again and we got a couple more siblings. We continued to move around. We never moved far away, so I only changed schools one time when I was ten years old.

All the moving around, rebuilding, divorces, relating to "new" mothers and other people, have of course, been influencing factors in moulding me. When I was fairly young, my father started to take care of foster children. These children usually had problems in school, with their parents or the law. This meant that we weren't a typical model family. We always had two to three foster children living with us. Some of the children were there for a few months and others for a few years. I have never doubted what is right or wrong. However, at such a young age, when one is in contact with criminals, drug abusers, kids with mental illnesses, drug addicted prostitutes and other good folks, it can't be helped that one would like to get their fingers in the pie, too. This gave me some experiences which, I think, only few are granted. I wouldn't want to offer my own children these experiences, but at the same time I wouldn't have missed out on them. I believe that what I learned from these extremely different people would normally take a life time.

Today it is easy for me to fit in with all types of people and new places. I am amazingly good at reading people and feeling what it is they need. I am very patient and flexible. I matured quite young and learned at an early age to take responsibility for myself and my actions. I can reep the benefits of these experiences now when teaching or conducting a course, for example.

At the age of eighteen I bought a summer house and moved away from home. When I was twenty I started my own craftsman business, had my first daughter and was the head instructor for a kung-fu school. Naturally, at the same time, I single-handedly renovated the house that we lived in.

In 1989 there was a repression in Denmark. So being self-employed was no bed of roses. Fortunately, I learned as a child to work. If I didn't do anything, I didn't make money. Yet, no matter how much I worked there was always time to train. I often had my little daughter with me. She would sit in a corner of the training center and play, or came with me if I worked on the weekends.

When I became a father, and thereby got the responsibility for another person, I began to think seriously about the meaning of life. This is when I started to get interested in Eastern Mysticism and the philosophy that is associated with it. I read hundreds of books on Taoism, Zen buddhism and a lot of other branches of these belief systems. Later I expanded my horizon with modern psychology and brain research, as well as literature on physiology and anatomy. During the course of this, I also became a Shiatsu masseur and participated in many courses, seminars, and lectures on subjects that could help me understand "us humans".

In this period of my life I really got around: Four children were brought into the world; I had between six and eight employees in my company which grew till I had a big, beautiful store. I was both the head trainer and the chairperson for an even bigger club and sat on the board of amartial arts union. I wasn't really interested in my job as a self-employed master craftsman but I didn't dare to think about it either. For someone who is self-employed it is hard to just change jobs and in this case it would have far-reaching consequences. So I continued to slave away.

After twelve years of marriage the cord finally broke. Whether it was because of too much work, that we had been too young or for a completely different reason, is not known, but in any case, our relationship stopped with all the emotional things that go with it. During the period that followed I pretty much just worked even harder at my job and in my training in order to get some distance from it all. Whether it was to come to terms with it or to run away from it, I never found out. It's just what happened.

I got into a relationship rather quickly after that and soon we had a child. Before long we threw ourselves into a huge house project which resembled, to a great extent, the place where I grew up: Total renovation from cellar to rooftop. Our second child came at a point when I was sick and tired of our house project and not to mention, my business. I went down with depression which made me think very deeply about my life. I knew that I had to stop my business. The last two years I could hardly drag myself around. It could be felt especially on our economy. In my deep, reflective state I found the answer. I must close down my business without too big of a loss and start some form of training center.

I presented my ideas to my girlfriend and she thought that it was definitely not good. Her opinion was that you know what you have but have no idea what you get. The bank shared her opinion. They would not support dreams!

For the first time I thought: Hell no, I won't do it! I would not let myself be controlled by others' attitudes and opinions. So I converted half of my store into a training room and cut down on the number of employees. All of this done without my girlfriend's or bank's blessings. I still had to work my fingers almost to the bone but I got out of my depression. Unfortunately, our relationship didn't make it through the upheaval. So there I stood with two failed relationships, six fantastic kids, a business I couldn't be bothered with and a dream that just wouldn't succeed.

The next couple of years was all or nothing and I succeeded in getting out of my business. I built up my training center to include martial arts, meditation, alternative therapies and diverse workshop facilities in very comfortable and nice surroundings where one can come and train and work on personal development. It was very hard economically. It had cost quite a bit of money to create this and the bank , as I said, never supported the idea. To believe that one can make a living as a karate master in a little provincial hole in Denmark is completely ridiculous. It was neither especially realistic nor well thought through, I will admit that, but I believed anyway that it could be done. I had fought and won before, both physically and mentally, on many different levels so why shouldn't this dream succeed?

One day in the summer of 2010 I had to go to a check up at the doctor's. He was to look at a mole that I had on my temple. He took a quick look at it and said that it didn't look so good. While I sat in his office he called a dermatologist right away who would take a sample from the mole. I got an appointment already the next day. In fourteen days there should be a result. I remember it was a Tuesday and that I was supposed to call after 10 o'clock for the test results. But, at precisely 9.55 my telephone rang. A different doctor introduced himself at the other end of the phone and said, "Yes... You, unfortunately, have skin cancer, but luckily only one out of ten die of it". Thank you very much! My world came crashing down around me. I didn't listen anymore to what he was telling me. It was just a hollow rumbling in the background. In that split second I was sure that I was going to die. What about my children? What would happen to them? And how should I tell them this news?

The next 24 hours were the worst in my life. I couldn't make heads or tails out of anything and paced around and around myself while I thought a million thoughts. After those hard 24 hours I was somewhat composed and clear in my head. I had decided that I wouldn't die. I had a dream. I had something to fight for. I wouldn't waste the rest of my life doing something that I didn't care to be doing. I would not use my time with people I really didn't like. I had never been more sure of which way I should go. No matter what would get in the way, I would continue in one way or another.

It's been three and a half years since I got diagnosed with cancer and I survived, as you can figure out. I am very thankful for the experiences I have had in my life and am, not least of all, proud of having gotten through what I have. Yet still I do think how sad it is that we humans have to get so far out that it's almost impossible to find our footing before we reach the core: that we have to be so pressured before we take the right decisions that support us in our dreams. We live a life where we content ourselves with what is good enough. We put up with too much crap and completely forget to sense ourselves - sense what it is we want.

I hope that this book can help YOU sense what you want. I hope that it will get you to look for your dream and then go for it. Don't wait until you are standing out on the edge because you know deep inside what you have to do. This book can hopefully give you a little push in the right direction.

I had decided that I wouldn't die.

Hell no!

Too often we do only what is expected of us. We follow along without really thinking about why: on the job, with our children, our parents, wives, husbands and other loved ones, in fact, with almost anyone we meet on our way. This is because we are so well brought up and full of consideration for everyone else.

But, once in a while, we actually have the right to object. We are allowed to stop and say "no!" Yet, in order to perform this manoeuvre, we must get in touch with our deepest feelings, look deep inside ourselves, to feel out whether we really want to or have the time to carry out others' orders, do favors for them or whatever it may be they ask us to do. If this is not the case, then it's about time to hold your head up high and say, "Hell no!", instead of letting others' wants and needs make you soft at heart and compromise your wants and needs.

It is actually a fantastically liberating thing to say "no", just once in a while, when putting others before us becomes chronic. It's liberating to object for our own sake, if we remember, however, not to involve our feelings. In combining feelings with a "no", the situation becomes an act of defiance and that is absolutely not purposeful. The only answer that is needed is just a simple, clear statement about the situation, right here and now. By far, most people would be able to accept and understand this if served in the right way.

However, it's not just other people we need to learn to say no to. We have to learn to say no to ourselves, for example, when we are lying on the sofa... again; or we haven't washed up or donethe dishes... again; and especially when we do all kinds of other things instead of what we ought to be doing. Procrastination. That's when it's time to step up and say: HELL NO! Say, "hell no" to being lazy and ineffectual! Say, "hell no" to being boring!

For just as much as we can use these words towards others, they are even more effective toward ourselves and our own lax and lazy habits and patterns of behaviour that we have built up over the years. The only thing that is required is to be a little tired of ourselves once in a while and, therefore, want to change some areas of our lives. When we can feel that one of these episodes is about to occur again, we need to put our foot down and say firmly to ourselves, "HELL NO!"

Once in a while, we actually have the right to say No!

Cheese with your Whine!

What in the world is wrong with human beings? What is happening to us? Even though we can barely greet each other over the refrigerated counter at the supermarket (where we buy unhealthy, half-fabricated food that we dare to call people-food) we find it terribly easy to dish out self-praise, exaggerations and lies while sitting, for example, in an overheated sauna at the swimming pool amongst half naked strangers we've never met before. We proudly tell these strangers all about our newly designed, super modern kitchens where we actually never use anything else but the microwave to warm up the above mentioned purchases; a detail that we, of course, don't bother to mention.

And after our little kitchen fairytale we naturally change over to boasting about our sports achievements, both running and cycling, several times a week. All the while, our somewhat plump bodies reveal a different picture than regular exercise. While the over-exaggerations drip down the hot plywood walls, the other sauna-goers nod their heads in recognition of what we are telling them before they themselves start on their lies of their perfect life, surrounded by the perfect framework, together with their perfect family.

However, we are not really listening, because we have much more on our minds. Still, in the suffocating heat of the sauna, we start to dramatically go on about how healthy we are, even though each putrid drop of sweat is evidence of massive waste being eliminated through our pores. We continue up the path of boasting and paint the prettiest picture of our very smart and talented children, who we, of course, always have time for. Even though we have a very demanding job with a lot of responsibility. And through this job, we are regularly rewarded for our unique contributions with promotions and fantastic job titles (which no one really knows what they mean). Of course, we can't get around not mentioning that with all these promotions we get bigger and bigger paychecks, so we're actually having a hard time deciding if our second international trip this year should be to Thailand, Bali or the West Indies. Naturally, we leave out the fact that, in reality, we are still trying to get our over-draught account out of the red zone after our last two trips. There's no reason to tell everything, right?

We finish off with the car (which also gets a thick coat of paint, so to speak), because, fortunately it won't be long before the sweet odour of new car interior reaches the nostrils and the sight pampers our vision. It's so beautiful that even our neighbor has to get a new one so as not to be left out. This is the neighbor we brag about knowing, among our huge and, not to mention rich, circle of friends who can get us so many things for much less than at cost price!

Why do we go to so much trouble to tell all this? When it comes down to it, we don't believe the story of the guy next to us so why in the world should he believe ours? What is it precisely that we are trying to achieve? Just because we say out loud what we really only dream about, doesn't make it more true. So why try to fool each other, and most of all, why lie to ourselves? Our lies do not become the truth just because we say them out loud.

Unfortunately, cultivating our image has become more important than cultivating ourselves. Apparently, our image must fit in with the norm, even though, in reality, none of us are able to live up to this picture perfect world of which we ourselves have helped to sketch the outline and contents. It can only be due to one thing: We are scared to death!

We're afraid of being inadequate. We are afraid of being a fiasco. Moreover, we are especially afraid that the people closest to us will find out who we really are: that they get down to our innermost being after peeling layer after layer off, until the only thing left is the truth... The truth about us as human beings.

Yet, there is no reason to be afraid, because, it is precisely there, under all those layers, where happiness hides... Real happiness, understanding, acceptance, and not least of all, love.

We are afraid of not going for it!

Energy

Energy is vigour: dynamic forces like a constant stream circulating throughout our bodies supplying our organs and cells with essential vitality of nourishment.

The word "energy" is synonymous with "life". Both concepts are necessary f o r the understanding of what body energy is.

Life is the sign that energy is present in our body. With lack of energy our bodies become sluggish, tired and depressed. With too much energy the body react s by becoming res t les s and hyperactive. When there is no energy, yeh, well, then we are dead! When energy, on the other hand, is in balance, we experience the harmony and well-being that we all wish for and deserve.

The body's energy level is regulated by the air we breathe, the food we eat, our sleep, heat, other people and our thoughts and feelings. Energy flows to where the attention is. If we are aware of just these factors then we can establish a balanced energy level relatively easily.

Another, and very important, place we can get energy from is through passion: Enthusiasm for what we are doing, when we are doing it. When we are together with enthusiastic people, their energy is contagious. No matter what they are enthusiastic about, we end up getting caught up in their good energy.

The difference between interested and enthusiastic people is that interested people want to know why things work while enthusiastic people want to know how they work. When we are passionate about something, time and space disappear, and we are able to keep the good energy stable over longer periods of time.

Find what makes you enthusiastic and you will find the source of everlasting energy.

Life is the sign that energy is in our bodies!

Dreams

Everyone has a dream: a dream of a better life. It's not necessarily because the life we have now is bad, but because we all have thoughts about certain improvements here and there.

Some people dream about big progress while some dream about small upswings. Some dream about freedom to do precisely what they want to, when they want to, while others "just" dream of a new car or a boyfriend or girlfriend. When it comes down to it, most of us actually achieve the many small goals we set for ourselves: The realistic goals, that are often based on what others think are realistic.

But most of the bigger dreams, visions and goals stay as they are; dream scenarios. We define them as being unrealistic in relation to what's normal, the norm, while the desire to follow those dreams still lives on inside of us. We suppress it only by justifying our reasoning while we navigate forward through our normal lives, in conformity with the rules we abide by. We are always ready to make excuses for why we can't pursue our deepest wishes.

Our dreams must be our bearings in this life, what we aim for. All too often, we have the tendency to lean back on the safety and security of daily life. We have a tendency to let daily life lull us into the old grind and bury us in triviality that is so far away from our dreams.

We never have enough time and always a hundred things to get done. But in our busyness we forget, all too often, that our dreams really come from a place deep inside us, a place we must not ignore. Dreams are our soul's song – a soul that longs for freedom, and a soul that won't be bound by rules and norms of how we should live our lives by reason, and a sense of reality as dominating values.

This is what Life ought to always aim for: an existence full of independent happiness and love; a love that can fulfill all your dreams.

The Meaning of Life

Imagine that the meaning of life is a boundless buffet of ideas and possibilities. It's all about trying out new ideas and thoughts without throwing any of them away before they are tried. For without change there is no progress. Without renewal there is no growth. As soon as you get new and better thoughts, let go of the old ones. If you do not get rid of the old thoughts, they will use you with their programmed habits and learned patterns of behavior.

We must understand that all of our problems are psychological problems. They don't exist outside themselves, so it's important to undertake a mental spring cleaning once in a while.

Among other things, you can do this by forming clear and concrete ideas about your present convictions. Why do you do what you do, and why do you believe as you do? In this way you can cleanse your mind and sharpen your perception.

It's important to be able to distinguish between basic shallow thought processes and deep thought processes. It is our innermost thoughts and attitudes that control our lives. If they don't support our wishes, dreams and goals, then the chance of reaching them are very small.

Most people are convinced that the conditions we live under and the life we have are strictly due to external circumstances. But the fact is, that in reality, our lives are formed by our thoughts.

Throughout history you will find a long list of documentation of people who have defied external circumstances, regardless of the extent, and thereby reached "the unachievable" goal through conviction and belief.

We human beings have the power to change our circumstances and create a meaningful and rich life. It is important, at the same time, to take responsibility for that life. Otherwise, we will fall back into putting the blame on everything else for our state of being and how it turns out. On the other hand, if we take the necessary responsibility for our own existence and create clear and distinct ideas for what we want with it, we will release an enormous amount of energy in our body and mind. Moreover, when we first learn to use this energy constructively, is precisely when we will stand with the key to health, freedom and happiness.

When we first realise that we can control the course of events in our lives, an enormous shift happens in the core of our body. In the beginning though, we are not quite aware of how to use this new knowledge. However, if we slowly begin to integrate it, carry it out in our actions, a change begins to happen.

Everything starts with an idea or a group of ideas. They help to lay down the conditions of our daily life. This is the creative plan. Whether you have to build a house or your own life, it happens in the same way: The visions you create internally, materialise externally. Disease and Old Age are mental ideas long before they become painful realities. Whether you create disease or good health depends on this factor: you create what you think about the most.

A mechanical engineer works in accordance with the same theory as the mental engineer. They are both dependent on the same creative intelligence. Mentally photographing with our brain creates the same picture as physically photographing with a camera. If we see a picture of an ugly thing, it can't suddenly become a beautiful swan. In the same way, our negative thoughts and ideas cannot bring positive results.

A lot of us experience that when we try to think positively, we are taken unaware by our own negative thoughts. These thoughts tell us that what we believe we are doing, will never succeed.

Other times we just throw away our ideas because we can't accept that our results are actually a product of our own convictions. We prefer to push the blame onto someone or something outside ourselves. Religion has been blamed a lot throughout history. There are people who even accept a life of disease, poverty and misery because their convictions tell them, that after a life of destitution, they will go to Heaven.

You create what you think about the most!

Our universe operates under a very precise law which we are all subject to. But mankind works with a limited degree of conscious awareness. Just because we don't completely understand the universal laws doesn't mean they don't exist.

Take, for example, an electrician. He works with electrical current and he understands how it is distributed and utilised. The electrician can control the current and create apparatuses and machines so we, the consumer, just have to push a button to get them to work. We don't need to understand how the apparatuses and machines work in order to use them. This is precisely the same principal that all science is based on, even the science of life.

It's important that we have the right attitude about always seeking the good in life and, at least, trust that we are on the right path, even though it sometimes looks as if we have lost and that our dreams have become fiascos. If it succeeds in the end, because you, with your creative intelligence held on to your goals, then it doesn't matter that there were bumps in the road now and then. Whether it is in your relationships, your health, your business or your economy that you desire improvements, you have the creative power inside you to achieve what you seek.

Through thoughts that support your goals you create the right vibrations, the right energy, which will lead you in the direction you seek.

To think, is a perpetual process. We can't just take a break. And whether we are conscious of it or not, we produce results all the time. Actually, we have the ability to decide for ourselves which results we want, just by regulating the form and quality of our thought processes. The goal is to wake up: To think our own thoughts and cultivate our own strengths, which is the most certain and reliable path to self-development.

Modern psychology has definitively stated that for every single change in one's life, there has to be a change in thought beforehand. It has been proven that the more undeveloped a mind is, for example, locked in habits and patterns of behavior, the harder it is to "wake up".

On the other hand, a developed mind creates higher individual viewpoints which have absolutely nothing to do with a higher education. On the contrary, an education can sometimes be a factor in limiting and locking the mind with its prejudiced convictions.

High ideas, tolerant attitudes, and healthy views are a sign of growth and development. No mind is too small to develop as long as we want it and are strongly convinced that it can be done. In this way, the path will appear in front of us as if we moved the camera and took a new picture.

Development and growth are a natural part of our lives. This planet we live on has a 15 billion year history. Its development and growth have always been progressive and continuously moving forward. We must realise that just like this planet, our intentions have always been, and still are, to develop our consciousness: In other words, to develop our mind into something bigger and better than it already is. When our intentions become the same as the universe, our development starts to take form, not for our own personal gain, but because we are a part of something bigger.

All mistakes in life are made because we let our external world control us, while all success is due to taking responsibility for our own life and following Nature's way. If we aren't willing to evolve, think differently and work with the fundamental laws of the constitution of life, then the law will not work for us.

We all have life energy in us. Everyone has the ability to create the life that He or She desires. With our thoughts and ideas we can plant seeds that will grow in our minds, as long as we understand life's fundamental laws.

The goal is to wake up: To think our own thoughts and cultivate our own strengths, which is the most certain and reliable path to self - development!

Focus

Once there was a young man who was very good at archery. Every day he trained at home in his garden, just because he wanted to. In the end he got so good that he hit the bulls eye every time. But it wasn't anything special for this young man. He did it for the fun of it.

One day, a stranger came by and saw this young man's fantastic ability. He asked the young man if he would like to participate in a competition with other excellent archers from the whole country. The prize was a very beautiful trophy, he would be in the newspaper and everyone would cheer him. This young man got so excited that he signed up for the competition right away.

The competition day was exactly one month from the day he found out about it. The young man was terribly nervous which he had never been before when shooting with his favourite weapon. But, because thoughts of winning filled his mind more than hitting the target, it didn't go so well on the day of the competition. The young man suddenly couldn't hit anything. Not only did he go home empty-handed, but his self-confidence suffered a terrible defeat.

The young man had two goals in his head: The target and the victory. It is undeniably difficult to hit two things at the same time. It is, therefore, important to keep your eye on the target and don't get distracted by other things, even though they might look absolutely brilliant.

In the same way as this young man had a hard time with having his cake and eating it, all of us have a hard time because we aren't able to focus. Instead, we latch on to what we think is smart at the present moment, or even worse, what others think is smart.

If and when we need to hit our target, we need to first know exactly what that target, or in this case, goal, is. Next, it's important that we make up our minds about what we can and will give up in order to achieve our goal. If, for example, we want to lose weight, then it is most likely that we have to avoid food that's fattening. Subsequently, we have to make the decision to go after our set goal. Finally, we need to act on it.

If you try to cut corners, as many of us certainly have tried a few times before, it will probably not succeed. Self-confidence and self-worth will diminish until, in the end, we think so little of ourselves that we completely stop dreaming and setting goals. We have to get back on that horse, focus on our goal and we are already half way there!

We need to know exactly what the goal is!

Fear

The most basic emotion of all is fear. We are all born with fear in us. It is a type of basic emotion that is intended to protect us from various dangers. This could be the fear of falling, fear of loud noises and the fear of being abandoned.

When we still lived in the wild, surrounded by untamed animals and other natural threats, this emotion was extremely constructive and helped keep us alive. Today, these dangers are no longer relevant for most of us. Nevertheless, the instinct is alive and well in so many people. According to psychologists around the world, the fears that dominate the most are the fear of not being good enough, fear of change, conflicts, rejection, decision making and, last but not least, taking responsibility. Even if we don't get anything constructive out of fearing any of the above mentioned situations, they control us all too much.

For the most part fear relates to the future. An expectation of something that happens later, a future we don't know yet, is what makes us insecure. If we fear something that lies out there in the future, it is completely impossible to handle this fear. We can never handle the future, but we can always handle the present.

Fear aids in creating and feeding the habits and thought patterns that actually stand in the way of achieving the success and happiness we dream of. We unconsciously build walls of lies and excuses around us, solely in an attempt to justify this unreasonable fear of not being good enough, being too old, too ugly, too beautiful, etc.. We build a secure and nice comfort zone around us.

We pass our habits and patterns on to our children. The simple words that a lot of parents use with the best intentions are, "Remember to be nice now". This actually prevents certain children from learning to trust their own feelings, as well as using and developing their intuition. These abilities help them to make decisions based on real, and most often, very different circumstances which, being nice, is not necessarily always the right approach.

Let's imagine we're at a party. Little Peter asks Uncle Andrew if he has drunk too many beers. Everyone, except the boy, become embarrassed and little Peter is reprimanded for saying out loud what everyone else was thinking. We often choose to show consideration or regard for others, even if it doesn't serve a purpose.

It's a disorder that has been given the appropriate term "pleasing disease", because it is a disease, an infection, that inhibits us from saying no, objecting and telling the truth. An infection that causes us to not dare to behave naturally for fear of hurting someone's feelings so they, or anyone else, won't like us anymore.

Fear does a lot to us purely on a physiological level. To live in constant fear leads to stress, which, among other things, makes our bodies mistakenly believe that the danger is so real that we either have to fight or escape to stay alive.

When our deepest primeval instincts get activated, our body automatically sends blood out into our arms and legs, leaving the organs with only a minimum of blood and nutrition. Every bit of energy must be utilised in order to survive at that moment, which is a fantastic ability to have... if we still found ourselves running around in the wild.

It's as if, though we no longer need these mechanisms in quite the same way as before, someone has forgotten to tell our bodies. And the body is just a servant that blindly obeys our emotions' commands. This means that our organs don't function optimally when we are stressed.

There is an old saying which says: *"Fill your own glass, before you serve others."* The words don't mean that we should be a bunch of egocentric individualists who are completely indifferent about anything and anybody around us. Instead, it means that we actually have such a high reserve of energy that you can help others. And it's not mere coincidence that it is recommended for a parent to put on an oxygen mask before their child's, in the case of a plane crash. No one benefits from a dead or unconscious parent! In actuality, if every person learned to think and take care of themselves first, then everyone would be thought of and taken care of!

Victim

"The taxes in this country are way too high! It is absolutely impossible to earn money in this system. And what about those teachers… do they think they can just goof off with short work days and long vacations?" "Ya, they should just be glad they even have a job! Just think about how much we others have to work to pay taxes so that these parasites can collect their fat pay-checks." "Yes, it's understandable that we neither have the time nor the money to live healthily. Just how in the world is it all going to end up?"

The characteristics of a victim are that they reproach, judge and complain. As victims we become people who suffer because of the actions of others. We become the ones who things get taken out on! At the same time as we take on the roll of victim, we renounce all responsibility because everything happens outside our reach. As a victim there is nothing we can do to change our circumstances or our surroundings.

If, for example, we want to lose weight and the undertaking of it doesn't work, an excuse often sneaks into our minds that supports us in thinking that, in any case, it is not our own fault that the needle on the scale didn't move in the right direction. But, they are just excuses that stand in the way of taking the required responsibility for our own progress. It's a pattern of justification that we started as babies. In order to weed out this phenomenon it takes a complete change in the way we think.

Isn't it funny how most people who, with great success, lose a lot of weight on a diet put it all back on again (and then some) shortly after? Or Lottery millionaires who use or lose all their winnings only five years after they received the money? These situations leave us with the big unanswered question of how to make our well-achieved successes last.

If we seriously want to change something in our lives we need to start from the inside, more precisely, with our thoughts. If we think like a victim the thought that we can do neither this nor that is the one that dominates. We can certainly go back to our childhood and maybe find the answer to who, or what, has done something to make us think the way we do and have the life we have. In situations where forgiveness is the main purpose, then going back might be useful. But in most cases, we don't have to look for answers in our past. We can't change the past anyway. On the other hand, we can change the present so that our future doesn't become a repeat of our past.

The characteristics
of a victim are

that they reproach,
judge and complain!

Forgiveness and Regret

Most of us walk around with unresolved grudges and distrust about someone or something; a feeling that hinders us from getting a clear sense of ourselves as we are. Yet, if we can learn to forgive, we can actually be released from carrying around these limiting feelings.

When we forgive, it's not necessary to say it directly to the person or persons involved. For it is not for their sake that we forgive. We just need to say it to ourselves, and while we say it, also feel forgiveness right down to our innermost core. In this way, we rid ourselves of these exhausting emotions which greatly limit our freedom.

To forgive does not mean we should tolerate inappropriate behavior. Neither does it mean that we should take up the relationship again with the person or persons we forgive. Forgiveness simply means letting go of the ties that bind us to the event. Never forgive for others' sake, only for your own sake.

Dr. Luskin, leader and founder of a project on forgiveness at Stanford University, said that people who have truly forgiven others, experience an immediate improvement in the cardiovascular system, muscles and nervous system: All of this without even delivering the message of forgiveness to the person or persons who have offended them.

In the same way, we can work with regret. It is easy to regret incidences or different events we have participated in in the past, that we find particularly unfortunate today. On the contrary, we become even more restricted by feelings of shame and guilt about our behavior. We achieve nothing by regretting anything. In principle, since regretting doesn't lead anywhere, we can just as well not bother.

When we regret something, as a rule, these feelings are an expression of anger that is directed towards ourselves. Thoughts have a habit of going round in circles without bringing any constructive results. It is very hard to get a sense of ourselves in the moment if, we find ourselves in a sea of angry thoughts that most often has to do with the past.

In order not to get caught up in these inappropriate patterns, we need to accept everything we have done in the past. Not regretting doesn't mean we don't learn anything from our mistakes. We are very capable of learning without bearing the shame, and the advantage is that we no longer let it weigh us down.

Like-mindedness

Some get the whole cake while others must make do with a single bite, or maybe even just a picture of a bite. Why is it that certain people constantly reach their goals while others always have to settle for less, change their objective or give up entirely?

All of us can recognise the above mentioned situation. Often times we make excuses to cover our failures while we put down the people who actually succeed. *"Ya, but she works all the time and hardly sees her family."* Or: *"He is with those kids way too much. It can't be good for them."*

We all have our own versions of complaints, such as: *"No, all that money? They must have cheated to get it."* Or, *"I certainly wouldn't want to live that fanatically. Life is simply too short for that. I've earned my red wine and smokes!"*.

Actually, most of us are so busy finding fault in others that we quite often search for others who are like-minded enough to do it with us. And so we sit and pat each other on the back while we agree that it's those who are rich and successful there's something wrong with. It's definitely not us!

In reality, it is us there is something wrong with, if that is the way we deal with our own lack of success and others' progress. It is just that form

of behavior, that makes it very difficult to mobilise the necessary energy needed to carry out a plan for a given goal.

To search for and find people who are similarly disposed, is in itself, a good idea. However, they should be people who support us in reaching our goals and not those who support us in putting others down. Putting others down only brings us further and further from our goals and dreams and makes us believe that it is hard to complete anything. And to believe we must, both in ourselves and in others.

We all have our own favourite excuses!

Changes

"Until one is committed, there is hesitancy, the chance to draw back, always ineffectiveness, concerning all acts of initiation – creation. But, the moment one definitely commits oneself, then providence moves too. A whole stream of events issues from the decision. Whatever you can do or dream you can, begin it. Boldness has genius, power and magic."

Johan Wolfgang Goethe

Nothing in the universe is constant. Everything is forever changing. Summer becomes winter. Night becomes day. Children become adults and so on. None of us can avoid this phenomenon. Yet, most of us always try to do what we usually do anyway, whether it's the christmas party, child-raising or daily routine.

Just like Nature, we, ourselves, are subject to these changes. Each and every second, millions of our cells are changed out in our bodies until the whole body is replaced after only a few years. It has been upgraded to a new version. Unfortunately, our behavior, habits, thoughts and patterns stay the same. We don't keep up with the development.

Without change there is no development! We cannot change the world but we can change ourselves. This sentence, I believe, most of us have heard a thousand times. We must change our perception of the world if we aren't satisfied with the one we have. It is our perception that actually creates our life. Even though I said that our bodies get upgraded to a newer version, it is through our perception whether this new version can be better or just a copy of the old one.

The responsibility for how our lives are formed and the responsibility for how we develop ourselves rests entirely on our own shoulders. If our perception of health is to eat poorly nourishing food, work under stress and not get enough sleep, then it's clear that our cells will develop in relation to these values. If you feel that life is hard and everything is against you then your cells will undeniably react according to this perception.

If you really wish to have a healthy and fit body, then you must do what it takes to get it. If you choose not to do this then you must accept the given results and don't complain, if and when, you still aren't satisfied. It's much better to be satisfied with what you have, than to be dissatisfied with what you don't have!

Normal versus natural

Is it normal to be natural? When it is normal to be a victim, is it natural at the same time, to be a victim of circumstances, surroundings, time and, yes, even life?

And what does it actually mean to be normal? Is it, I wonder, a democratic process where the majority decides? Is it a process where we automatically get categorised in relation to other people so that we can be sure about which group we belong to, and how we should behave in order to stay within what's normal?

When are we then natural? Do we really know at all or have we just forgotten it? We often hear people say that a certain person is "natural". Does that mean that the person hasn't had any plastic surgery done or that the person doesn't use make up? Maybe we need to go all out and live in nature to be "natural". Shall we live in a "Nature" where, in our part of the world, it has become so immensely difficult to spot in its original form because we human beings have massively left our mark in the form of industry, farming, forestry, infrastructure, parks and the like?

It's been a long time since humans pulled themselves out of the equation called "Nature": The "Nature" having to do with balance and cycles. It's the "Nature" that we get so much from without appreciating it, except by filling it with nothing but garbage and pollution as gratitude. We forgot a long time ago to give back, which "naturally" helps influence our way of thinking and, thereby, our lives.

Everything in the universe is made of energy: An energy that stagnates if we don't send it back into circulation. Take, for example, our body, which must be said is the most natural thing we have. It vibrates with energy and we have to feed it with good, nutritional food, a lot of sleep, fresh water and happy, positive thoughts, in order for us to have a healthy and fit body in return: One that supports us in our daily life and in reaching our goals.

If we, on the other hand, treat our body like we have treated Nature for so long, it will limit our development. By now, we all know, all too well, which results we get by serving bad, prefabricated food, stress, angry and negative thoughts for a body that is supposed to last a whole lifetime.

What we want in our lives is also what we must give. If we want, for example, to have wealth and health in our existence then it's a prerequisite to have a rich and healthy way of thinking. If not, then we will never get what we want most.

It's been a long time
since humans

pulled themselves out of
the

equation called
"Nature"!

Consciousness

The human being has two forms of consciousness: Subconscious, which constantly works with our programmed habits and patterns, and the waking consciousness which is active when we are actually conscious.

To be able to see clearly, and especially to be able to see what we consist of inside, we need to be conscious. Many of us live by habitual standards and routines, which is fantastic, when we find ourselves in traffic, for example, and have to react quickly. However, all too often, the habits are allowed to take over our life instead of supporting it, which to a great degree, shuts out our consciousness.

Consciousness is a muscle which must be trained just like everything else. The more we train, the more conscious we become. There are many ways in which we can train our consciousness, for example, through meditation and breathing exercises.

There is, though, one step that we must go through in order to actually be able to begin to work with our consciousness. This is to acknowledge that we need to expand our level of consciousness. We have to admit that we need to change some things if we want to move onward, upward and outward. It's easy to be conscious of others' mistakes and shortcomings, but we cannot take away our own headache by going to our neighbor and giving him a pain killer. We can't change the world but we can change ourselves!

In order to get started, we must look inwardly without judging ourselves. We must observe what we see and afterwards slowly begin to reveal who we really are. It is there that we can first start to change. We have to get to know ourselves, for it is when we know ourselves that we can change ourselves, not when we just think that we know who we are.

Without the use of consciousness we sink, all too often, into a swarm of thoughts and stress. When those thoughts are first allowed to roll through our heads, it is no longer easy to have control over anything: Focus disappears and we steer randomly through our lives without any sense of direction.

If we use our consciousness, on the other hand, and work towards increasing it, we help ourselves in getting where we actually want to be. Lack of consciousness holds us fast in our present situation. Consciousness heightens the senses and keeps us razor sharp in relation to our own thought patterns, until we are gradually able to choose precisely which thoughts work with us and support us towards our goal.

Consciousness heightens the senses

and keeps us razor sharp!

External Influences

We are all influenced by our surroundings: Our family, colleagues, neighbors, sports buddies and so on. But we are also influenced, to a great degree, by the media!

The average person sees and listens to different kinds of media between five or six hours a day. I am talking about television, radio, computer and not least of all, mobile telephones.

Think about it, that just four hours a day adds up to two months a year. Seen in this perspective, it's quite a long time to spend on it.

It's absolutely right to keep well informed, but we don't need to let ourselves get flooded with everything that comes out on the airwaves which, so often, is classified as entertainment: Entertainment which, unfortunately for many people, is taken seriously, as if it were on the level of meaningful journalistic work.

To let yourself be entertained is fine, as long as we know that this is what is happening. When we first begin to let this entertainment influence us and actually develop ourselves in accordance to the values of what lies behind it, that's when it gets dangerous.

We often forget to use our critical senses and form our meanings and attitudes according to what we see and hear through the media. If nothing else, it is important to be critical. It is, despite everything else, our lives that this is about! Most people, if not all, can think for themselves. But we find it hard to keep our integrity intact when, day in and day out, we get bombed from every side by what most often has completely different interests in mind than to inform, develop and help us to reach our goals and dreams.

When all is said and done, we are the only ones with an actual responsibility to ourselves. So, instead of just sitting back and letting ourselves be entertained, we should actively and consciously search for information that will benefit our development.

To let yourself be
entertained is

fine, as long as we
know that this is

what is happening!

Imagination

As children we had big dreams about everything we wanted to do in our life time. There were no limits to how wild and fantastic these dreams were. Everything was possible!

But, suddenly, one day we begin to turn our focus on everything that could go wrong instead of keeping focus on our dreams. We became "realistic".

However, to be realistic and sensible is the biggest killer of them all, when it comes to ideas and initiatives. As children everything is possible, there are no limits. This realistic and moderate life philosophy we ascribe ourselves to as adults, influences most of us, and therefore, also our way of setting our goals.

We organise our mindset in relation to our assumed sense of reality. We even begin to defend our new, reasonable ideas. At the same time, we degrade our dreams as being childish and just a product of a lively imagination, even though they are still smouldering inside us. They lie there waiting to get the chance to jump out and become reality.

Yet, all too often we choose instead, to live a mediocre life and "be content" with what we have: "Because it's good enough and we'd better not think that we are better than we are!"

However, as Albert Einstein already pointed out many years ago, "Knowledge leads us from A to B, while the imagination leads us everywhere". So the challenge is that we must get out of that rut and start setting new and exciting goals.

We must not be modest, but use our imagination in grand style. The doors are wide open and the shelves are full!

It's only our own self-limitations that stop us. So aim high. As Michelangelo once said, "The problem isn't actually that we aim too high and don't reach our goals, but instead that we aim too low and reach them". That is to be content!

We must not be
modest, but use our

imagination in grand
style. The doors

are wide open and the
shelves are full!

Frequency

Everything in the universe is made up of energy. Everything has a vibrating energy field. Even a stone on the beach has molecular oscillation which can be seen under the right microscope.

All energy vibrates with a frequency and when something has the same frequency as another, they get attracted to each other.

When we, for example, tap a tuning fork, all the string instruments with the same frequency within a certain radius will begin to vibrate. And if our radio isn't quite tuned in to a definite channel, then all that comes out is crackling sounds from the speakers.

In order to attract something in particular, we have to copy the right vibrations, feel the rhythm and emotion in every cell of our body, as if we already stand in the middle of our dream. If our belief system supports us, then that which we wish for will come so much easier to us.

As an example: If we feel that we are not good enough, then we have a very hard time attracting anything that is good for us, because our mindset does not support our desires. We think we do not deserve it, and therefore, attract the opposite. All self-reproach inhibits us in manifesting that magnet which only attracts good things to us.

If we have an automatic will, a will driven by our subconscious mind, then we cannot sufficiently mobilize the strength to manifest our wishes and desires.

However, if we want to piece things together, even a little bit, and desire to attract something different and new in our life, then we must begin with stimulating our will to want something different and new. It's when we first have a conscious will that we can create the power, the magnet, to fulfill our desires.

We have to copy
the right
vibrations,

feel the rhythm
and emotion in

every cell of our
body!

What can YOU do?

Do you ever think that you actually are your own best friend? It's you that has to motivate, encourage and tell yourself that "you can do it". It is you, that when life looks most bleak, has to lead yourself back on track so you can see the path in the dark.

You have to have the deepest and strongest trust in yourself. If you, of all people, don't believe in YOU, then who will?

Of course, you should be around people who support and believe in you. Moreover, you should be with happy and positive people whose behavior rubs off on you. Even so, if your own inner voice doesn't back you up then your life will be one uneven and unworthy fight.

If you create an "inner" resistance towards yourself, then you will run up against it time and time again "outside" yourself. The frequency, the vibrations you send out, will reflect your inner voice.

You become the master of your life when the voice within you suddenly gets louder and clearer than the world around you.

You must be present and attentive when you are with other people, both privately and at work. When you are present in what you are doing, the results will be much better and more satisfying for you. You must practice every day being in the moment and giving attention to those around you.

Train by breathing deeply into your stomach and ask yourself every day how you are. Give your body everything it needs in the way of healthy food, sleep and exercise, so you are always fit and ready for the daily tasks.

You decide yourself how you want to react to different situations. You can actually choose to be happy and positive no matter what. You get nothing out of being angry and negative.

If you smile a little more, you will quickly discover the positive energy that springs up around you. You must laugh as much as is humanly possible and surround yourself with positive and joyful people. Then life will be much easier to handle.

It is life-affirming to give. You always get it back in return and even more. If you give people a little more than they expect then you have already made a very good connection.

People are created to give, which doesn't mean that you shouldn't receive, for that is just as important. You should pass on the good energy and in this way create more growth around you.

There is no reason why everything has to be so serious. Once in a while it's good to just let go and go with the flow... of life. You must play more and not just when children are around, but in all aspects of life. Life flows better when we play, which doesn't mean to be childish or naive but tobe curious and experimental. In this way, new situations will come up all the time so that life isn't just a treadmill of trivialities that we run around in.

Remember that you are the creator of your own masterpiece. It is you who stands at the rudder. So set the course towards what you want out of life, towards what gives you meaning and happiness. Don't waste your life fulfilling others' wishes and expectations. Follow YOUR dream.

You become the
master of your
life

when the voice
within you
suddenly

gets louder and
clearer than the

world around
you!

One Thing at a Time

When stress rears up and let's itself be known and you can't handle anything, when everything feels unmanageable and nothing in your life seems to function as it should, then it's time to slow down.

When we get stressed our bodies are too. It works under this condition with a very limited rational thought process and reasoning. A stressed body has two choices: It can either fight or flee. There is no room, at all, for any type of long-term planning; it's all in the here and now, but absolutely not in the good zen way where we are consciously present in the moment. On the contrary, in this state we are behind with everything, for the most part, while we cling to the wish of being far into the future where everything has miraculously fallen into place.

This form of life conduct does not prolong our lives. Moreover, to get out of this vicious circle we have to work at reducing the pace/tempo by simply settling for doing one thing at a time.

Most might say that we can only do one thing at a time, but that's not true. We humans have a tendency to do many things at a time, in our heads, which naturally can't be done in the practical sense The body doesn't actually know this. It just follows the boss's, i.e. the head's, messages, for a while at least.

We're thinking all the time that we have so much to do, while at the same time, we naturally have to be in great shape, bake our own bread, look good and be the perfect parent. We simply have way too much going on and the mistake in this lies in that we are so busy trying to justify our existence with a lot of external things, that we have clearly forgotten our health and happiness in the process.

But, the good news is that by doing one thing at a time, we can actually and easily get back again to the state where we begin to be aware of ourselves and our own needs. We can get back to the state where we can manage our wonderful life, get rid of the stress and find the true joy and happiness that we all deserve.

Try, once in a while, to turn off the telephone, "pull the plug" and steer clear of daily business. Nature is a fantastic place to go when we can't manage anything at all. Get out and experience it and come back with renewed energy and strength.

Love Yourself

Do you love yourself? If not, the probability that others don't either is quite big. If you don't love yourself very much then the energy you send out will influence other people and their perception of you.

It may be that you experience people's pity, but you will never be able to get their full acceptance and respect if you don't accept and respect yourself! Consciously or unconsciously you seek their acknowledgement and sympathy. This can often put people off because they feel that you drain their energy. On the contrary, if you care about yourself then you will attract people with the same high energy which will lift you even higher.

To love yourself in this context isn't meant as an egotistical act, where you don't give space to others, and you are always right. This only means that you fill your own cup first before you fill others', so that you have lots to give without being drained

Self worth is love for yourself, and self worth is an ingredient in reaching your goal in this lifetime. The more self worth you have, the greater the goal you can achieve and the more goals you can seek. At the same time, you will be more at ease with yourself and show more selfconfidence in all situations. You will not be nervous or afraid to try anything new, but instead, throw yourself into exciting projects

without speculating too much or worrying unnecessarily.

Although it does gives you support, you won't need other people's acknowledgement and/or words of praise, because you can do it yourself! You won't even really have the need to brag about your accomplishments. Why brag about something naturally achieved when you have already thrown yourself into the next exciting project? The truth is that if you don't love yourself you can't really make use of your full potential. You will have a difficult time finding out what you really want out of life. If you actually do find what you seek, then you won't dare follow it because, "it will never work anyway".

Love for yourself is the decisive factor of whether you achieve the goals you set for yourself or not: Whether you can fulfill your dreams. You are your own source. When you completely learn and understand this you will never run dry!

Summary

- Say no when you realize, that others are crossing your borders.
- Say no to your own bad habits.
- Appreciate what you have and stop regretting what you haven't got.
- Do not lie to yourself.
- Provide your body with the required nutritious food drink and sleep.
- Spend time with enthusiastic people.
- Find your passion – what makes you enthusiastic.
- Make room for your dreams and do not oppress them.
- Remove indifferences from your life.
- Think about what you think.
- Your life is formed by your thoughts and what you think about the most, you create.
- Find your goal/goals in life and aim your focus there.
- Do not please others.
- Let not your fear control you. It's just a feeling you have created yourself.
- Your life is your responsibility and no one else's.
- Stop whining.

- Forgive everything – regret nothing.
- Do not judge.
- Do not try to convince everybody.
- Find those who support you in reaching your goals.
- Understand that everything is changing.
- Break free from the norm and find your natural way.
- Sharpen your senses – activate your consciousness.
- Put extra effort into everything.
- Turn off electronic devises – turn to silence – live in the now.
- End realism and jump over the edge.
- Feel your dream and sense the energy.
- Become your own best friend.
- Be the friend you have always wanted.
- Stop and feel – are you going in the right direction?
- Do one thing at a time.
- Summon all your love – and give it to yourself.

Exercises

Introduction

The following exercises help to bring you into balance both physically and mentally so you get a surplus of energy and an overview of your life.

Before you start the exercises it is important that you really make time for doing them. Make sure that you will be undisturbed for the breathing and meditation exercises. Read the whole text thoroughly before you begin so you are sure you understand what you are supposed to do.

Devote time to develop yourself every day!

Breathing

Natural breathing happens through the nose. In this way the air has the right temperature and moistness when it reaches the lungs. At the same time, the biggest dust particles are caught by the nose hairs, that is, if the hairs haven't been removed by laser treatment.

It is extremely important to breathe all the way into the stomach, which means that you have to use your diaphragm.

In this way, not only does more oxygen get into the blood but also more blood gets cleansed with each inhalation. Your intestines get massaged from the inside, as well, so that your digestion improves.

On the other hand, if you breathe only into your chest, you get less oxygen per inhalation and, instead, your heart must beat harder in order to distribute oxygen throughout the body. If the body doesn't get enough oxygen to work with, it is already stressed.

Breathing Exercise 1

o Sit on a chair with your back straight with both feet on the floor, and your hands on your stomach. In this position practice breathing deeply into your stomach.

o Relax your shoulders while you breathe in and feel how your stomach distends a bit outward.

o When you breathe out, either through the nose or mouth, relax the whole body. Your breathing should not be strained, but naturally and effortlessly.

Do the exercises several times a day until it becomes natural to breathe this way. You will experience more energy and well-being. Feel how your general condition and health get noticeably better.

Breathing Exercise 2

- Sit on a chair with your back straight, both feet on the floor and hands on your lap. Breathe deeply into your stomach and relax your shoulders.

- Now count while you breathe out, either through your nose or mouth. Remember to relax your whole body throughout the exercise.

- Count to five each time you breathe in. Count to five while you hold your breath. Count to five while you breathe out and then count to five as you hold your breath, before breathing in again.

- Continue to do this exercise for two to four minutes.

This exercise should help you to be able to control your breath so that you don't go into panic, for example, in stressed situations.

Awareness

To be aware is the same as being intensely concentrated, where, with being present, you have your focus on one thing at a time.

To have focus on one thing at a time means that you become more meticulous and make an extra effort, which, in the end, gives a much better result than if you tried to multitask your way through life.

A concentrated mind is not an aware mind. Whereas a mind that is aware can be concentrated. Consciousness or awareness never shuts out anything; it takes in everything.

Conscious awareness sharpens your senses and clears your head.

Internalized Awareness Exercises

Direct you full attention towards yourself. The points below are only suggestions. You can add more if you like. Do as many of the suggestions as possible every day. The results will be much better.

- o Affirm yourself with words, thoughts and feelings.

- o Stand naked in front of the mirror and enjoy what you see without trying to find faults and short-comings.

- o Your inner voice should be positive and supportive.

- o Do something that you know makes you happy.

- o Eat and drink healthy things.

- o Do only exercise and physical activities that you find enjoyable.

- o Sleep well and enough.

Awareness Exercise 2

Direct your full awareness toward your food for a week. All food and every drink you ingest in this week must be done with the greatest awareness.

- o Taste your food as if it was the first time you ever tasted it. Don't judge the food, just taste it.

- o Chew the food thoroughly.

- o Take the chance to taste something completely new. If you, for example, eat take out food, then choose something you've never tried before. Break habits.

- o Make at least one meal yourself that you haven't attempted before.

You should count on setting aside more time for making your meals in this week. In return, your body will quickly experience a lot of satisfaction for the care and consideration you show it by giving full attention to the fuel you pour into it. Because you won't eat as fast as you usually do and probably not as much as you are used to, this exercise will benefit both your physical as well as your mental well-being, and, because you will better utilise nutrients in the food.

Bon Appetit!

What you think is what you create!

Meditation

Meditation means to reach down to your core through conscious presence of mind. To reach the core means to reach into the soul, the ego, the higher self or whatever word you feel fits best. It requires work to reach the core, but along the way, you will experience marked improvements both mentally and physically. These improvements will show themselves in the form of being able to concentrate better, sleep better and less stress.

You don't need to use a whole lot of time to meditate. In the beginning you can just sit for five to ten minutes, once or twice a day, when it fits in with your schedule. In just a few weeks you will experience a big improvement. The goal is not to sit and meditate for thirty minutes twice a day, every day. Like the breathing exercises, the goal is to be able to get into the meditative state wherever and whenever you wish.

Breathing Meditation

Find a place where you will be undisturbed. Turn off the telephone and remove anything else that could make distracting sounds.

- o Sit on a chair with your back straight. Place both feet on the floor and your hands on your lap.

- o Breathe through your nose and down into your stomach. Every time you exhale say to yourself "relax".

- o When you are completely relaxed direct your attention one hundred percent towards your breathing. Observe it as if it was the only thing that exists.

- o If thoughts sneak into your consciousness, just look at them, let them go and go back to your breathing.

Gradually, as you keep your attention on your breathing, you will increase the time until you can sit undisturbed for about ten minutes.

Sequence of Numbers Meditation

Find a place where you can be undisturbed. Turn off the telephone and remove anything else that could make a disturbing sound.

- o Sit on a chair with your back straight. Place both feet on the floor and your hands on your lap.

- o Breathe through your nose and down into your stomach. Each time you exhale say to yourself "relax".

- o When you are completely relaxed direct your attention one hundred percent towards your breathing. Observe it as if it was the only thing that exists.

- o Begin to count your breathing. Count each inhalation and each exhalation until you get to nine, then start again.

If you can't remember which number you have come to, or you have counted too far, then just start over. If thoughts sneak into your consciousness, just look at them, let them go again, and return to counting your breaths. Gradually, as you keep your attention on counting the sequence of numbers and breathing without being disturbed, the time will increase until you can sit undisturbed for about 20 minutes.

Learn from the past, prepare for the future, but live in the Now!

Alfa State

People's brain waves oscillate with a certain frequency, depending on what is happening and what state they are in.

The waking conscious state for adult people is called beta state. It is on this level that we, for example, can learn and execute different work assignments, in other words, being aware of our surroundings. When we, on the other hand, give ourselves over to deep sleep, which is necessary for us to feel fresh and rested the next day, we are in theta state.

Just before we slide into that sleep level, we go into alfa state. This is the same level as when we are waking up. In alfa state we almost let go of our physical body. We find ourselves in a state where we can communicate with our subconscious where our habits and patterns of behavior are stored. It is precisely at this level that we have the possibility to change that which is no longer beneficial for our present dreams and desires.

In the end, through practice, we can ourselves, consciously choose to move from beta to alfa state. This can, among other ways, happen during meditation.

Alfa-meditation

Find a quiet place where you won't be disturbed. Turn off the telephone, radio and other disturbing elements. Be sure that you can sit undisturbed for 15 minutes. You must sit on a chair with your back straight and both feet on the floor. Rest you hands on your lap.

- o Start by saying loudly to yourself, "In 15 minutes I will come back to full consciousness".

- o Close your eyes and breathe in slowly on a count of four seconds. Hold your breath for two seconds and breathe out slowly on a count of four seconds, while you say out loud, "relax". Repeat four times.

- o Breathe calmly and relaxed throughout the rest of the meditation.

- o Every time you exhale count down from 50. In other words, the first time you breathe out you say out loud, "50"; the second time, "49" and so on, until you get to zero. It is important your thoughts don't wander and that you focus on your breathing.

- o When you are finished with counting down in sequence you will be in alfa state. Here you can begin to talk with yourself internally.

- o Mention everything you are thankful for and all that you desire in life. Say it as if it has already happened. For example, "I am glad and thankful for being in perfect health", even if you may be sick right now. If it is material things you wish for then say that as if you already have them, "I am happy when I drive around in my red Ferrari with my beautiful wife in the passenger seat".

- o Be concrete and add as many details as possible.

- o Wish precisely what you want and believe in what you wish for. You can wish for the same thing every day and you can wish for something new each day. You decide yourself.

- o When the 15 minutes have gone by your body will tell you and you will automatically open your eyes.

To get the best results, you must meditate every day, if possible. Once in the morning and once in the evening. It may be that you don't reach alfa state in the beginning, but, be patient.

It can be a good idea to write down what you are thankful for and what you wish for before you start meditating.

Good luck with the rest of your life!

It's not how you start but how you end!

"It may be that things take longer than you planned, but if you give up, you will never make it."

-Per Nygaard

Inspiring authors:

Anthony De Mello

Lao Tzu

Brendan Burchard

Bob Proctor

Jim Rohn

Bruce H Lipton

Greg Barden

Bruce Lee

Bob Doyle

Neal Donald Walsh

Michael Beckwith

Dalai Lama

H. C. Andersen

Karen Kingston

Sanna Ehdin

And many many more……………